every book,
every page,
SOMETHING
happens!

A Gift For: Kindergarten
KS

Given By: Tayler James

Printed in U.S.A. © 1997 Scholastic Book Fairs, Inc.

Scholastic
Book Fairs®

D0536872

$2

Pa Grape's Shapes

by Phil Vischer

Tommy NELSON™

Thomas Nelson, Inc.

Nashville

Art Direction:
Ron Eddy

Lead 3D Illustrator:
Aaron Hartline

3D Illustrators:
Thomas Danen, Robert Ellis,
Joe McFadden and Joe Sapulich

Render Management:
Jennifer Combs and Ken Greene

Published in Nashville, Tennessee, by Tommy Nelson™,
a division of Thomas Nelson, Inc.

Library of Congress Cataloging-in-Publication Data
Vischer, Phil.
    Pa Grape's Shapes / by Phil Vischer.
        p. cm.
    Summary: While searching for new tires for his car, Pa Grape
encounters a variety of shapes, including a triangle, rectangle, and
crescent.
    ISBN 0-8499-1507-4
    [1. Shape — Fiction. 2. Stories in rhyme.] I. Title.
PZ8.3.V74Pag 1997
[E] — dc21
                                        97-27852
                                            CIP
                                            AC

Printed in the United States of America

97 98 99 00 01 02 03 BVG 9 8 7 6 5 4 3 2

Dear Parent

We believe that children are a
gift from God and that helping
them learn and grow is nothing less
than a divine privilege.

With that in mind, we hope these
"Veggiecational" books provide years
of rocking chair fun as they teach
your kids fundamental concepts
about the world God made.

– Phil Vischer

President
Big Idea Productions

This is Pa Grape. He loves the outdoors!
He loves what God made —
    all the mountains and shores!

He'd like to go visit the stuff he admires.
But look! His old car doesn't have any tires!

This is Pa Grape and the thing with the screen
Is his Robo 2000 New Tire Machine!

"It's really quite easy," says dear old Pa Grape.
"To get a new tire, just pick out a shape!"

"But I can't remember — oh, dearie! Oh, me!
What shape does a tire for my car need to be?"

"Maybe a triangle! That ought to work!"
And the box springs to life with
a groan and a jerk —

triangle

And spits out a tire not too big, not too small,
That just sits on the ground — without rolling at all.

"Oh, dear," says the grape. "That's not good,
    that's not good!
A tire should be rolling! I know that it should!"

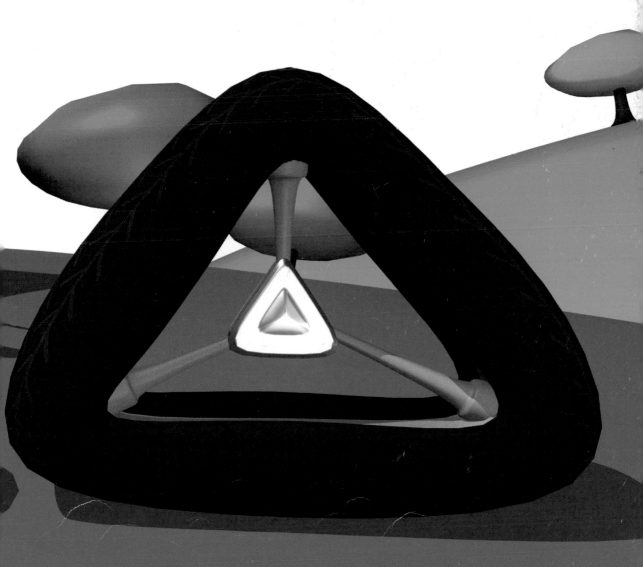

"Let's try a square! Oh, that's a nice shape!
I think it's just right for my car," says Pa Grape.

The square hits the ground
with a big, heavy thud.
But roll it does not. Pa yells out, "What a dud!"

"I'll try a rectangle, just to be fair."
But it doesn't roll any more than the square!

rectangle

"Here's an idea — I'd bet my new sweater!
Maybe a shape that is round will roll better!"

So Pa tries a crescent. "The back part is round!"

crescent

But once it rolls over, it sticks in the ground!

"Maybe an oval! It's round all the way!"

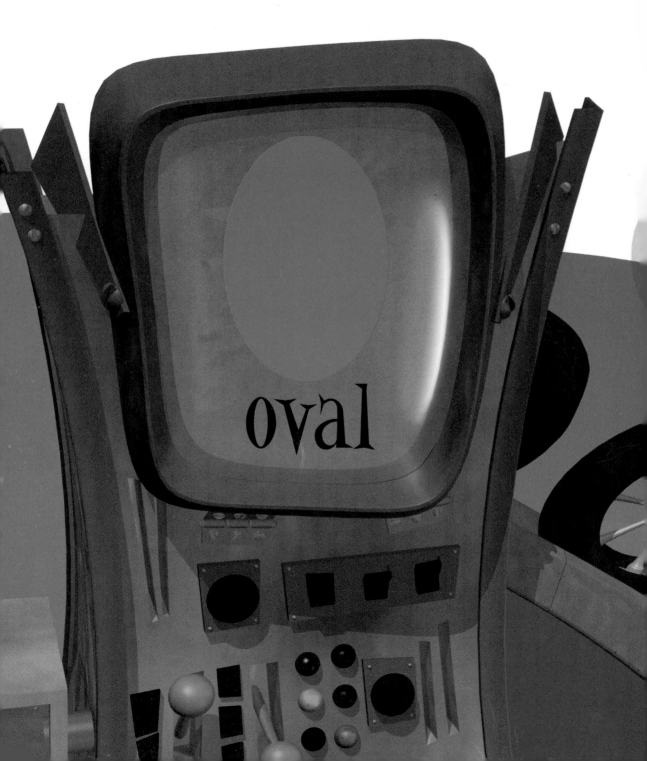

oval

And out pop four ovals.
  "They're rolling! Hurray!

I guess if it rolls it just *might* do the trick —
But that wibblin' and wobblin' will make us all sick!"

Now, here is a circle. The very last shape.
"It looks quite a bit like a ball," says Pa Grape.

circle

"Hey! Balls are good rollers,
    I know that it's true!
So maybe a circle will roll nicely, too!"

At last, the new tire appears on the ramp.
It looks like a dream, and it rolls like a champ!

"It's perfect!" cries Pa. "Oh, so smooth and so round!
The tire for my car I have finally found!"

"Only one thing left to find now, I guess …
I need a good friend to help clean up this mess!!"